The ultimate business skills collection from Bloomsbury Business

The new *Business Essentials* series from Bloomsbury Business offers handy pocket guides on a wide range of business topics – from writing a CV and performing well in interviews, to making the most impactful presentations, finding the right work/life balance, brushing up your business writing skills, managing projects effectively, and becoming more assertive at work.

Writing Skills for Business
How to communicate clearly to get your message across

Manage Projects Successfully
How to make things happen on time and on budget

Assert Yourself
How to find your voice and make your mark

Succeed as a New Manager
How to inspire your team and be a great boss

Balance your Life and Work
How to get the best from your job and still have a life

Give Great Presentations
How to speak confidently and make your point

Get that Job: Interviews
How to keep your head and land your ideal job

Deal With Stress
Improve your health through changing how you work

Get that Job: CVs and Resumes
How to make sure you stand out from the crowd

Available from
as well

BLOOMS

Balance Your Life and Work

How to get the best from your job and still have a life

BLOOMSBURY BUSINESS
LONDON · OXFORD · NEW YORK · NEW DELHI · SYDNEY

BLOOMSBURY BUSINESS
Bloomsbury Publishing Plc
50 Bedford Square, London, WC1B 3DP, UK
29 Earlsfort Terrace, Dublin 2, Ireland

BLOOMSBURY, BLOOMSBURY BUSINESS and the Diana logo are trademarks
of Bloomsbury Publishing Plc

First published in Great Britain in 2004 by Bloomsbury Publishing Plc
Revised edition published in 2009 by Bloomsbury Publishing Plc
(under the A&C Black imprint)
This revised and updated edition published in 2022 by
Bloomsbury Publishing Plc

A catalogue record for this book is available from the British Library

Library of Congress Cataloguing-in-Publication data has been applied for

ISBN: 978-1-4729-9321-2; eBook: 978-1-4729-9322-9

2 4 6 8 10 9 7 5 3 1

Text design by seagulls.net

Typeset by Deanta Global Publishing Services, Chennai, India
Printed and bound in Great Britain by CPI Group (UK) Ltd, Croydon CR0 4YY

To find out more about our authors and books visit www.bloomsbury.com
and sign up for our newsletters

Contents

1
What's your work-life balance like?

Juggling lots of commitments means that life today has never been busier. Whether you have family commitments or not, it can sometimes seem hard to fit everything in – we all want to be successful at work and yet have time for ourselves. Work through these questions, to assess your work-life balance, then read the guidance points.

How much of your time does work take up?

a. I let work take up as little time as possible.
b. A fair amount – but I still leave time for myself.
c. Work seems to dominate my life.

What position does work hold in your personal life?

a. Once I'm out of work I forget about it.
b. I do spend some time thinking about work while I'm not there.
c. I think about it constantly.

How often do you find yourself getting swamped by tasks?

a. Never.
b. Occasionally.
c. Often.

How often do you find yourself getting stressed at work?

a. Almost never.
b. Occasionally.
c. All the time.

Be honest! Which of the following best describes you at work?

a. Over-relaxed.
b. Balanced.
c. Workaholic.

Do you feel you have enough time for yourself outside work?

a. Yes.
b. Most of the time.
c. No.

Do you feel like you are in control of your life?

a. Yes.
b. Just about.
c. No – I feel I'm being swept along by work.

Are you happy with where you see yourself in three years' time?

a. No. I'd like to have accomplished more at work than I think I will have.
b. Yes.
c. No. I'd like to have more of a life outside work than I think I will have.

a = 1, b = 2, c = 3.

Now add up your scores.

8–14: You seem to have plenty of time for yourself, but are you fulfilling your potential at work? Take a moment to work out what is important to you and make sure you're on track to achieving it – Chapters 2 and 3 provide advice on this. Creating a list of priorities for the future can help you to set goals for yourself and ensure you don't miss opportunities. Some time away from the office may help you work out what you want to do. Turn to Chapter 6 if you're thinking about a career break.

15–19: You appear to have struck a healthy balance, putting in the effort at work while still having the time for 'normal' life. In order to keep this balance and take your work and life in the direction you want, it could be worth creating a plan to make sure you get where you want to be. Turn to Chapter 3 for help on this. To keep up the good work, Chapters 7 and 8 will help you prioritize and prevent stress building up.

20–24: Your work seems to have swamped your life. Sit down and take stock of your position, and assess what's important to you. Chapters 2 and 3 will help you work this out. You can then move on to plan how you can change aspects of your life and claw back some time for yourself. Chapters 4 and 5 can give you some advice on this and Chapters 5 and 7 can help you to become more efficient, making your work life a better place to be.

2
Weighing up your current work–life balance

'Time flies when you're having fun' goes the adage. Time also flies when you're very busy – but rather than having fun, you can soon find yourself stressed in a way that affects not only your mental and emotional well-being, but your physical health. When there isn't enough time in the day, something has to give: but is it to be your work or your personal life? Achieving a balance has become one of the burning issues of the day.

Here are some of the main reasons why more and more people are addressing the topic of work–life balance:

The COVID-19 pandemic made many people reconsider their priorities in life.

More pressure and longer hours at work mean people 'burn out' younger.

Government figures show that although Britain has the longest working hours in Europe, our workforce isn't as productive as those in some countries with shorter hours. So while people are spending more time at work, they aren't necessarily achieving more.

More people living longer means that a growing number of workers care for elderly relatives.

The broad argument for greater balance and flexibility at work is that greater satisfaction among employees will lead to fewer stress-related illnesses, less time taken off for sickness, lower staff turnover and higher productivity.

People with a good balance between their work and other responsibilities and interests tend to be more motivated and productive: in other words, happy people work better.

Step one:
Understand what the concept means for you

The ideal work–life balance is a very personal concept. It isn't an obvious, tangible or static thing that people can identify, get right and then expect to keep. It's dynamic and has different elements for different people at different times.

Work–life balance is sometimes confused with finding ways to work less or to work flexibly, because for some people these are the most important elements of a good balance. As a general concept, work–life balance is a feeling of being in control of your life, being able to exercise choice and about finding an equilibrium between your own needs and those of others, whether at work or at home.

If you're unhappy about the way things are for you at the moment, don't worry; there's a lot you can do to help yourself. The first step is to pinpoint what being in and out of balance is like for you and to understand the triggers. Once you've worked out those, you can move on to find a solution.

Step two:
List your symptoms of being out of balance

To work out a way to move forward and get your life in kilter, it's a good idea to first look back at how you've felt in the past.

✓ Take a sheet of paper. Remembering the last time you were really out of balance list some words that describe what you felt. For example, you may have felt as if you were spinning out of control, chaotic, panicky, stressed, shattered or ill.

✓ List how people at work would have described you during this period and the behaviour they might have noticed at that time.

✓ Now list how your family and friends would have described you during the same period.

✓ Do the same for each out-of-balance episode you can remember.

Step three:
Find out what triggers an out-of-balance state for you

Think back through the episodes above when you felt out of balance and narrow your focus down. Ask yourself:

- What happened to start each out-of-balance episode?

- Was it an action you took? If so, what triggered that action?

- Was it an external event? If so, what were the first signs of the event?

When you've done this for all the episodes from step one, review your triggers. Are there common themes? For example, did you feel out of balance when your boss put too much pressure on you? When you had a row with your partner or with a close friend? Were you already out of sorts before that?

TOP TIP

Close your eyes and take some deep breaths.

Imagine breathing out all the negative or stressful thoughts that you've been remembering. Take a break before moving on to step four.

Step four:
Work out how you feel when you're in balance

Perhaps surprisingly, describing being in balance is not always easy. It changes according to who you are, what's happening and when.

✓ Take another sheet of paper. Remembering the last time you were really in balance, list some words that describe what you felt. How will you recognize that feeling again?

✓ List how people at work would have described you, the behaviour they might have noticed during this period.

✓ Then list how your family and friends would have described you during the same period.

✓ Do the same for each in-balance episode you can remember.

Step five:
Find out what triggers an in-balance state

✓ Now review each of these pleasant periods and try to identify what happened to start each period. Ask yourself:

✓ Was it the result of an action you took? If so, what triggered that action?

✓ Was it the result of an external event? If so, what were the first signs of the event?

✓ When you've done this for all the episodes from step four, review your positive triggers. Are there common themes?

TOP TIP

It's good to feel in control; some people call it 'being in the zone'. Whenever you think that sensation is slipping and you need a lift, close your eyes and remember how you feel when you're in the zone. See if thinking about one of the positive triggers helps you tip you back into your balance zone.

Step six:
Work out how you feel at the moment

Now you've identified what the ends of the spectrum are like for you, you can 'map it out' in a simple table or grid. Add descriptive words from steps one to five in the bottom line, as you'll see in the example below.

Totally in balance	Tipping in	Neither in nor out of balance	Tipping out	Totally out of balance
In tune with myself and family, happy, relaxed, confident, generous with my time, proactive.	Kind to myself, take time out, even cancelling work, make more time for family.	Indecisive, reactive, not very kind to myself, perfectionist, OK with others.	Unkind to myself, don't rest, take on too much, pile on the pressure, snappy with my kids and partner.	Hate myself, rude/ unfair to others, exhausted, defensive, ill, no sense of humour, depressed.

When you've put in your own descriptive words for each part of the spectrum, you can identify the 'box' that best describes your current state. You can use this personalized tool to tune in regularly. If you are tipping out of balance, you'll find that you see the warning signs earlier; this will help you to take some remedial action before things get really difficult to deal with.

**Step seven:
Find your locus of control**

One of the key themes in work–life balance is your locus, or centre, of control. Again, this isn't a static factor but one that can be changed by beliefs and by events. When people feel in control, they can 'make things happen' and psychologists have shown that feeling in control is associated with a better sense of well-being. When people feel like this, they're said to have an internal locus of control.

When people feel controlled by others or by events, things are happening to them and they're said to have an external locus of control. They're more likely to feel anxiety and loss of confidence, and report physical symptoms of stress. In the extreme, an external locus of control can lead to a long-term state of helplessness and depression.

A locus of control is best thought of as a ratio, because it isn't the same across all situations. To identify whether your locus of control is generally internal or external, keep a diary for a week. Each day, think back over the different stages, tasks and meetings of the

day and identify how in control you felt. You need to
suspend your logic; what you are doing is honestly
recording how you felt. Here's a worked example:

Part of day	Internal: I was making things happen	External: Things were happening to me
Getting up	✓	
Taking children to school		✓
Getting to work		✓
Organizing my day		✓
Meeting with staff	✓	
Responding to clients		✓
Solving problems	✓	
Part of day	Internal: I was making things happen	External: Things were happening to me
Lunch	✓	
One-to-one with boss		✓
Out on client site with boss		✓
Picking up children		✓
Making tea	✓	
Going to the gym	✓	
Bath and bed	✓	

In this example, the person recording their locus of
control has a 50:50 ratio. As we don't know what's
right for that person, we can't tell if that ratio in this
case is good or bad. What you need to do, once
you've worked out your current ratio, is plan what

you'd like it to be in the future. For example, you may be comfortable with different ratios at work and at home. If so, which ticks would you transfer between columns?

TOP TIP

Review the steps above and make a list of what you would like to change for the future. Carry this list forward to the next chapter, to work out your priorities.

Common mistakes

✗ You feel trapped

If you allow yourself to believe that you can't change anything, you're ignoring a huge array of everyday choices that you make through habit alone. Suspend this belief while you go through these exercises, deciding instead what you would like to change 'if you could'.

Allowing yourself to visualize the future you want is an incredibly positive exercise. By the time you've worked through the steps in this book, your belief will be more along the lines of 'I choose to...' – you'll be making things happen.

BUSINESS ESSENTIALS

✔ Work-life balance means different things to different people; what's right for you might not be the right thing for others, even those you're very close to, such as friends, family or your partner. Don't make any assumptions about the right balance for other people; they need to work it out for themselves.

✔ Work-life balance is also dynamic; the right balance for you will change as you go through your life.

✔ If you're a manager and you're worried about the work-life balance of one of your team, talk to them about it. Listen carefully and don't leap in with advice or jump to the wrong conclusion when you have no evidence.

✔ Learn to recognize what being in balance or out of balance means to you, so that you can quickly take steps to remain in your personal balance zone.

✔ Understand what triggers different states of balance for you. This will help you to predict periods of stress and work on contingencies in advance.

✔ Assess your current state of balance regularly and work out what you'd like to change. This increases your locus of control and by being proactive, you'll stay in your comfort zone.

3
Working out your values and priorities

In Chapter 2 we looked at how to assess your life balance and having done that, you should have a clearer picture of what is working for you currently and which areas of your life you would like to change. You also have a better understanding of what being in or out of balance is like for you, and this will help you recognize the symptoms early and take steps. Hindsight is wonderful. It's relatively simple to look at the past and even the present and say what is right for you now. It's harder to look forward and decide what balance will be right for you next week, next month or next year.

Knowing what the balance is that you're aiming for and trying to maintain is the starting point. The steps below will help you to break down what the factors are and to organize yourself according to their relative importance to you. In fact, what will be right for you tends to change, so you need to make time to check it and adjust it if things have changed. Add a 15-minute check in your diary every week until it becomes a habit.

Step one:
Work out what's important to you

Divide up a page into the following areas:

- me
- partner/family
- work/career
- finances
- friends/hobbies/leisure
- health

Write down the things that you feel passionately about in each of these areas. You may find that there are a lot of overlaps, and you may also find that some boxes have lots in while others have very little. Don't worry about this – there are no hard and fast rules.

Real-life example 1

Me: Earn respect. Be loving. Don't hurt others. Space and downtime for me. Learning and growing. Time to sit and think. Recharge the batteries.

Partner: Love. Two-way support. Time together. Teamwork. Atmosphere.

Work/career: Earning. Integrity. Professionalism. Collegiate atmosphere. Challenges. Lots of interaction with people. Building something for the future. Being respected. Having a good reputation.

Finances: Earning enough to be comfortable. Planning ahead. Investing wisely where possible.

> Friends/hobbies/leisure: Lots of interaction with people. Holidays with others.
>
> Health/fitness: Good physical appearance. Good mental health.

If you find this difficult to do, here's another way of getting at your values:

● Close your eyes, imagine yourself at a much older age, looking back at your life. First, imagine that you've had a really full and satisfying life. Take a sheet of paper and write down the things that you're proud to have done. What were the best bits that give you joy to remember? Now imagine that you're looking back over a wasted life. What do you regret and what do you wish you had done more of?

> ### Real-life example 2
>
> Time and energy well spent in a full and satisfying life:
>
> My family: Time spent talking, communicating with them, helping them develop, just being together, loving and being loved. Building solid friendships for love, sharing, support and learning.
>
> My business: Created something bigger than myself, developed great understanding of clients' needs, developed new ways to help. Helping others. Developing myself to understand others better.
>
> In a wasted life I would regret:
>
> Not travelling and learning about other cultures. Wasting time on appearances rather than substance. Lost contacts with family and friends. Staying

employed all my life for the 'security'. Wasting my
creativity. Harming others or failing to help where
help was needed and I was able. Poor health as a
result of not looking after my body.

Step two:
Translate these thoughts into a single list of your values

✔ Write, in a couple of words, the essence of each of
the thoughts you've listed in the previous exercises,
with no repeats. Sometimes two or three of your
original thoughts might be summarized under a
single heading.

TOP TIP

Values are very personal and so are the definitions
that we use. Don't worry too much about the words
that you use here; other people may interpret them
differently, but that doesn't matter.

The important thing is that you know what you
mean by a particular label.

For example, the labels you could use are:

- love and fun;
- respect;
- harnessing thought and creativity;
- development and support (self and others);
- communication and interaction;
- earning/being productive;
- helping others;
- building for a better future.

Step three:
Work out the relative importance of these values to you

Values tend to be hierarchical, which means that you can prioritize them. As the next step in the process, rank your values in order of their importance to you.

TOP TIP

For you to get the best out of the exercise, don't allow any values to 'tie' (that is, be joint first, joint second and so on); the list has to be a real rank in order of importance.

For example:

1. love and fun;

2. respect;

3. building for a better future;

4. helping others;

5. earning/being productive;

6. development and support (self and others);

7. communication and interaction;

8. harnessing thought and creativity.

✓ To check that the order you've chosen is right for you, ask yourself: 'If I have value no. 1 (in this case, love and fun) in my life, will I have value no. 2 (respect)?' And so on down the hierarchy.

✓ If the answer is 'yes', then they're in the right order for you. If the answer is 'no', try a different order, until each pair feels right.

TOP TIP

It may seem that logically your values might not be linked in this way, but try to suspend your logic while you try the step above.

Values are internal and sometimes irrational, but there is a 'natural' order to them. Clarifying the hierarchy of your values is a very powerful step in helping you to prioritize in a way that is more satisfactory for you.

✔ The second check is to start at the bottom of the hierarchy and ask: 'Does value no. 8 (harnessing thought and creativity) support and contribute to value no. 7 (communication and interaction)?'

Because the relationships between the values are based on your beliefs about living, others may not find them strictly logical or make any sense of them. As long as they make sense to you, though, you'll derive benefit from them.

Remember that your beliefs are built up from a very young age as you learn from your experiences. As you work through this exercise, you may experience moments of insight about why certain elements of your life balance are the way they are. For example, if you shared the values displayed in the examples above, you may find that your great drive to 'build a better future' is fuelled by the belief that this will contribute to 'respect' and therefore allow you to 'be loved and have fun'.

Step four:
Set yourself some goals

Now you need to bring the results of the exercises into the real world and translate them into positive action.

✓ With your list of values in front of you, ask yourself what you'd like your life to be like in three years' time.

✓ Write your answer in the positive present tense, making sure that your answer is as fully descriptive and as positive as you can make it.

You may end up with three or four bullet points for each value. Some of these may be statements about things that you regularly do, others may be specific qualifications achieved or goals met. Include how you'll feel about your achievements.

For example:

Value: Love and fun

The family eats together most evenings and we chat about our day and our plans freely. There are lots of laughs and genuine contact between us. We set aside time for homework and encourage the children through our example, sitting down with them where possible. At weekends I spend plenty of time playing with the children and finding new ideas or environments to introduce to them. We also allow them time without direct supervision. My partner and I make time to relax together and just be in each other's company, whether with friends or alone.

or

Value: Interest

I go for lots of walks with no pressure of time at weekends and enjoy the house and local countryside. I feel really fit and in tune with the seasons. I can consider investment projects and get through the reading I want to do. I spend lots of time on creative things, such as painting, music and socializing.

> **TOP TIP**
>
> Don't forget to include elements that you identified as things you wanted to change when you worked through the exercises in Chapter 2.

When you read back through your three-year plan, it should feel inspiring. When you read it, it should make you feel, 'Yes, this is what I am working towards'. If it doesn't, go back through your values and see which is not fully implemented in your plan.

✓ Once you're happy with the three-year statements do the same for one year's time. Bear in mind that three one-year plans must add up to the three-year plan.

✓ Next, plan for six months' time, again in the positive present tense. Remember to make this realistic and in tune with the one-year plan.

✓ Finally, write your one-month plan. You could turn some elements of this plan into a diary, if you find that helpful.

Make sure that you're as positive, clear and descriptive as you can be about what you've achieved by the end of the month. Be careful about the goals you set, though, and plan in advance how much progress is 'enough'.

There are only 24 hours in a day and you may not be able to fit everything in. Remember to give yourself a break even as you work towards achieving your goals. If you don't think your plan is realistic, think back over the long term. Ask yourself:

- Which opportunities are only available now?

- Which things can take a back seat for the moment without negatively affecting my life balance?

TOP TIP

The 3-1-6-1 plan is very powerful and can act as a fantastic motivational tool, too. As you work through the steps, you'll become very clear about, and very active in, the choices you're making and this will help you feel more in control of your destiny and your balance.

When you feel your motivation dipping or your balance slipping, refer back to your plan and review the choices you've made. Are they still right for you or should something change? Remember that the plan's not set in stone; it's just a way of laying out what you're hoping and working for. Make it flexible so that when you change (as we all do), your plan will also change. Review the plan each month and write the next month's.

Common mistakes

✗ You confuse other people's values for your own

When we're young, we learn a lot from our parents, siblings, teachers and other people with prominent roles in our lives. We also take on others' values. Later, as we become more independent, we may test and throw out some of what we've learnt and we go through a transition period during which our adult 'persona' is formed. Adults often carry with them the 'voices' of important others, reminding them of 'musts', 'shoulds' and 'oughts' and sometimes people find these useful.

Be aware of these voices as you go through the steps in this section. Do you really agree with them deep down? Are they still helpful to you? Or have the 'oughts' and 'shoulds' become tyrannical, pushing you to do things that aren't resonant with your values? Watch out for times when you use these words and ask yourself if they're coming from within you or from others. Are they right for you?

✗ You don't take into account other people's needs

Although the process outlined above focuses mainly on you and how you think and feel about things, do check in regularly with the important people in your life as you work through it. Perhaps they'll want to think about their values, too, so that you can see which are truly compatible and where important differences lie. Don't see this as a threat to your relationship with them, but rather as a way to help you to appreciate each other's positions better in the future. Your plan may very well require support or direct input from these people, so it will be important to see whether your plan takes their needs and timings into account. For example, if you have a family, the plan has a much better chance of working if you're all on the same wavelength than if you're all planning in different directions.

BUSINESS ESSENTIALS

✓ Values are the motivational elements that drive our actions and reactions. They're built up throughout our lives and have been shown to work hierarchically. Knowing the relative importance of your values can give you great insight into why you act and react the way you do.

✓ Create a plan that includes the elements you need to have in balance. Setting goals around these elements draws you towards the future you would like.

✓ Others have an effect on our values and on our plans. Don't forget to talk to those who share your life.

4
Working more flexibly

Chapters 2 and 3 covered how to assess how you feel and what your main priorities are. We'll now look at some of the options open to you to improve your balance and the quality of your life overall.

The good news is that people are much more aware of the importance of a good work–life balance than ever before, and achieving it doesn't mean that you have to change your life radically: it's all about modifying the way you work in order to accommodate other responsibilities or aspirations. It doesn't only apply to parents of young children or people who need to care for dependents, but all of us.

Flexibility in the workplace is being driven by business need; not only are working cultures and attitudes changing in many parts of the world but also the COVID-19 pandemic forced both businesses and employees to rethink what worked for them. A good deal of employers recognize the need to adapt if they are to recruit and retain the best people. In short, then, you're an asset and your company will want to keep you!

Step one:
Find out about the options open to you

Employees now have the right to take periods of paid maternity, paternity and parental leave, as well as the right to take time off (either paid or unpaid, depending on circumstances) to care for dependants. There are, however, several other key areas in which you can address your work–life balance needs and preferences. These are:

Flexi-time working

People working on flexi-time schedules are able to vary their start and finishing times, provided that they work a set amount of hours during each week or month.

Flexi-time is not only great for parents trying to manage a household as well as a job, but also for anyone who finds working within a strict and continuous routine depressing and demotivating. Everyone's energy levels fluctuate during the day but not necessarily at the same time, so flexi-time helps enable people to work at their peak. Both those who work from home and in an office/workplace can benefit. City-workers and commuters can use flexi-time to avoid rush-hour – probably one of the most time-wasting and stressful parts of the day.

Part-time working

Employees with a part-time arrangement may decide between working fewer days each week or fewer hours a day.

This option also works well for people with parental or caring responsibilities. The other people who benefit greatly from part-time working are those returning to work after looking after young children, those recovering or suffering from illness and people who are trying to pursue other interests or careers.

> **TOP TIP**
>
> Part-time working should be attainable without you becoming sidelined in the organization or losing benefits, such as sick pay and holiday pay. If you're concerned about this, you can find out more about your rights as a part-time employee online (try gov. uk/part-time-worker-rights).

Job sharing

This involves two people dividing a full-time workload between them, with each working on a part-time basis. This is beneficial if you want to maintain your career while being able to spend more time with your children or to pursue other interests outside work.

Working from home

The COVID-19 pandemic accelerated a shift to working from home for many employees, especially those in offices and call centres. Many office-based companies learned that productivity was not affected by employees being at home and, in many instances, it improved. Hybrid work weeks, allowing employees to split their time between home and the workplace, are now becoming an established part of working life.

This style of working is a boon for parents and carers, but is also valuable for people without those kinds of domestic responsibilities: it allows them to work more productively, especially in tasks that require a great deal of concentration, and uninterrupted peace and quiet away from colleagues, phones and day-to-day admin. It saves employees both time and money, by reducing commuting and the costs of office clothing and work lunches. Employers can benefit by reducing the amount, and therefore cost, of office space.

Term-time working

This option allows employees to take time off work during school holidays in order to look after their children. This time off is usually taken as unpaid leave, although the salary can be paid evenly across the year. The sorts of employers most likely to operate this scheme are those in industries that experience seasonal peaks and troughs.

Other options

The variety of opportunities being adopted by organizations to help you achieve the right balance doesn't stop there.

The UK government's website (gov.uk/flexible-working) is a great place to find out more about the options available. In addition to the ones outlined above, the following exist:

- staggered hours: staff work to different start, finish and break times;

- compressed working hours: staff work their total weekly number of hours over fewer days;

- annualized hours: staff have more flexibility about taking time off as working hours are calculated over the year rather than by the week;

- shift swapping: staff negotiate their working times and shifts between themselves;

- self-rostering: staff state their preferred working times and then shifts are organized to accommodate as many of those preferences as possible;

- career breaks: as well as paternity, maternity and parental leave, staff may also be allowed unpaid career breaks and sabbaticals;

- time off in lieu: staff are given time off when they've put in extra hours at work;

- flexible and 'cafeteria' benefits: staff are offered a choice of benefits so that they can pick those best suited to them.

Step two:
Make an application for flexible working hours

How the process works

Most people apply for flexible working because of their family situation. However, at the time of writing, all employees in the UK have the right to request a flexible working arrangement, not just parents and carers. (NB The rules are different in Northern Ireland.) Employees must have worked for their employer for 26 weeks (so six months) before making a request.

✔ Check the employees' handbook or with your human resources department (if you have one) to see what the preferred method of application is. If there is nothing established then follow the steps for making a statutory application below. Bear in mind that only one application can be made in any 12-month period.

✔ Do some informal research. Once you've checked out your company's policy, speak to friends or colleagues who have applied for flexible working hours or who are already working under a new arrangement. How did the successful applicants approach their request? Are they finding it easier or harder than they'd anticipated to work in a new way? Bear in mind that if your working arrangements are changed, these changes are permanent unless otherwise agreed between you and your employer.

✔ Make a statutory application

1. Write to your employer with your request.
2. The employer has up to three months to consider your request, or shorter/longer as agreed with you.
3. If agreed, your contract will be changed to reflect your new working terms and conditions.
4. If rejected, your employer must write to you explaining the business reasons behind the decision. Employers are expected to deal with all requests in 'a reasonable manner'.
5. You may then take your case to an employment tribunal if you feel your request has not been treated fairly.

Make a persuasive case

 Prepare your case and try to anticipate the questions your manager may ask you when you meet to talk about your application. Requests can be turned down because managers fear that flexible working arrangements may affect the business, so be prepared to give well-thought-out, positive responses to questions such as:

● Will you still be able to be an effective team member?

● How would a change in your working hours affect your colleagues?

● What will be the overall effect on the work you do?

● How could a change in your working hours affect the business positively?

TOP TIP

Be realistic and also be ready to compromise. A popular way of approaching negotiations of any type is to draw up a wish list for your successful outcome that contains an ideal solution, a realistic one and an absolute minimum. If you show that you're prepared to be flexible, your manager may be willing to meet you halfway.

 Think about when you would want any new arrangement to start and give your company as much notice as you can. This will convey the fact that you're still committed to the company and are thinking about how the potential changes to your working life will fit in overall.

Stress that the quality of your work and your motivation will not change, even if your working hours do. In fact, you'll be more productive as you'll suffer from less stress and will need to take fewer days off sick to look after your children or dependants when they're ill.

You could also explain that as part of a reciprocal arrangement whereby all parties benefit, you'd be willing to work extra or longer hours in times of heavy demand. Finally, but no less importantly, explain how much knowledge and expertise you've built up while you've been working there and how much the company benefits from it.

TOP TIP

Many companies or organizations will allow you to bring a union representative with you to a meeting to discuss your application. If you do invite one along, make sure he or she has read a copy of your application and any related documents from your place of work so that he or she is up to speed.

Follow up

According to the gov.uk guidelines, you should be informed about the outcome of your application within three months of your meeting, or according to a timescale they agree with you.

 If all goes well and an agreement is reached, your new working arrangement and an agreed start date should be set down in writing and copies given to all relevant parties (you, your manager and the HR department or representative if you have one).

✓ If your request isn't granted, you may appeal to an employment tribunal. See the gov.uk website for further advice on this issue.

Step three:
Set up a flexible working system in your organization

If you're an employer or manager, be prepared for some extra administrative costs involved in, for example, setting up IT equipment at home for employees who usually work in an office or other work location. However, the benefits of retaining skilled and experienced staff should outweigh these costs, not least in reducing the expense of recruiting and training replacements for dissatisfied employees who leave.

Think about the needs of the business

Start by clarifying the most important needs of your business. Flexible working will only be sustainable if it doesn't hinder your business's ability to perform efficiently and profitably.

✓ Speak to your staff to find out how many of them are interested in exploring flexible working arrangements.

✓ Engage staff in thinking about how flexible arrangements would affect the business and customers. Discuss what sort of reorganization might be involved in new working arrangements.

✔ Ensure that your staff understand what the business needs from them, so that they don't make unrealistic requests about working flexibly.

TOP TIP

If you're an employer worried that your business won't be able to cope if all the employees decide they want to work flexible hours, you can relax. By consulting with your employees before new arrangements are introduced, you can avoid resentment developing and ensure that flexibility works to everyone's advantage.

Develop and implement a policy

✔ Formulate a policy on how your business views flexible working. Discuss these ideas with staff as you formulate them, so that they see the policy developing and feel they've been consulted in the process.

✔ Write down a procedure for how you'll deal with requests for flexible arrangements and how staff performance will be monitored. Make sure everyone is aware of these procedures.

✔ Implement your plans over a trial period.

✔ Together with staff, review how well the process works and assess the impact of flexible working on the business.

✔ Make necessary changes to your policy or practices; monitor and review these regularly.

TOP TIP

As an employer, the key to making flexible arrangements work is setting and monitoring the workload and tasks for employees. If proper trust is established and workloads or tasks are agreed and monitored, there should be no need for direct supervision.

Common mistakes

As an employee:

✗ You don't prepare well enough

As with all types of negotiation, you need to make sure that you've done your groundwork when you make an application for flexible working hours. First, be aware of your rights by researching the issue: you might want to visit the gov.uk website or the equivalent in your country, which sets out the rights and responsibilities of both employers and employees. Second, check your company's stance on the issue, making sure you follow the procedures properly when submitting a written application. When you meet your manager to discuss the application, stress that your commitment to your role and the company will not change, and think through questions he or she might ask you about the effects of flexible working on your workload and that of your colleagues.

✗ You aren't flexible

Bear in mind that the legislation relating to flexible working hours gives you the right to request them; it doesn't mean that your company will necessarily agree to your application, although they have a responsibility to consider it reasonably. If you're flexible when you meet with your manager and open to compromise if your ideal scenario isn't possible then it's much more likely that you'll end up with a result that suits everyone concerned.

✗ You don't think through all the financial implications

Don't forget that when you reduce your hours, it's not just your salary that may be affected. Pension contributions and other benefits may change, too. Be sure that when you take the decision to apply for flexible working hours, you'll be able to cope financially if your application is granted.

As an employer:

✗ You try to implement a cultural change too quickly

Moving towards a work-life balance, and bringing about a cultural change for the better, doesn't happen overnight. You should strive initially to create an environment of openness and mutual respect, where individuals gradually begin to feel a growing sense of support and trust. From there you can move towards striving to achieve a proper balance between the demands of your business and the personal needs of your employees. This will give them the opportunity to contribute fully at work while also being able to fulfil family responsibilities or whatever private needs are most important.

✗ You begrudge employees who want flexible working arrangements

Employees who make choices that support a work-life balance shouldn't feel a sense of disapproval, nor that they can no longer expect to progress within your organization. It's important to be inclusive and to avoid alienating people with particular personal needs.

✗ You have insufficient contact with out-of-office staff

Staff who aren't in the office regularly may start feeling isolated. You should try to avoid this as a manager, by planning regular feedback meetings either by video call or in the office, and organizing social events to bring staff together from time to time.

BUSINESS ESSENTIALS

✔ Research shows that flexible working arrangements can be introduced without damaging a business. There's a clear business case for getting the work-life balance right, as people work better when they're happy with their working conditions, and high turnover costs caused by the loss of skilled staff can be reduced.

✔ When assessing your work-life balance, decide upon your career aims and personal ambitions and how long you think you need in order to achieve them.

✔ Find out about all the various flexible working options available. Consider which one would suit the needs of your desired lifestyle best.

✔ An application for flexible working needs to be well researched. You should prepare your case thoroughly so that the employer feels reassured that you have the business's best interests at heart as well as your own.

✔ Employers should take a planned approach to implementing flexible working arrangements in your business, involving consultations with staff to decide on the best policy and process.

✔ Flexible working policy should be implemented over a trial period and followed up with a review of how it's working and adjustments to ensure that the business continues to function efficiently.

5
Juggling family and work demands

Whether you're part of a couple or not, as soon as you have children, many aspects of life are brought into sharper focus and some important decisions have to be made. You need to know how to move forwards and you have to be sure that your work–life balance will allow you to enjoy your time at work and at home.

Working out who is responsible for childcare, household chores and earning income are the three most obvious decisions required, but they're not necessarily the easiest or most clear-cut ones to take. This chapter takes you through the steps required to work out the best options for you. Once you know what these are, talk to your boss or HR department about changes you need to make happen at work. To find out more about current employment rights around taking time off for family and dependants, visit gov.uk.

If you have a partner, you'll reap most benefits if you both think about the exercises below; it doesn't matter if you work through them at the same time or if you do them separately and then compare notes at the end. Whether you're parenting together or alone, these steps will help you to identify the benefits and risks of different ways of managing your career alongside your family life.

Step one:
Identify the advantages and the demands of work

✓ Start by thinking about your current or most recent work role. Make a list of what the benefits are for you and your family, such as:

● income;

● social interaction;

● feeling valued for a worthwhile professional role;

● keeping career progression going;

● keeping skills up to date.

✓ Next, identify the demands of having such a role. For example:

● requirement to work 40 hours per week minimum, whether from home or in a location/work venue;

● an understanding that you may be prepared to work 60 hours per week when it is busy (sometimes this is an expectation that is inherent in a company's work culture, rather than a written element of your contract);

● paying for childcare;

● giving the job all your attention and energy during working hours;

- a certain amount of socializing with clients outside office hours, when required/possible;

- weekend preparation time;

- commuting if you don't work from home. Depending on where you live, this may be up to as much as three or four hours per day;

- making sure you're completely up to date with current trends and markets.

TOP TIP

Although it's easiest to start with current or recent roles, try to think more broadly now about other work roles that you could consider with your current skills and strengths. Most people will stick with what they know, but if the demands outweigh the benefits it would be worth considering other possibilities that are open to you, rather than feeling trapped. Are the demands and advantages broadly the same for other roles or are some quite different?

Thinking over these issues may help you find a new work area where you could have many of the same advantages that you have now, but with fewer or more manageable constraints.

Step two:
Identify the demands of family and home

Thinking about your roles in the home as parent, spouse, homemaker, entertainer and educator, what will be the major demands on your time, energy and resources? You may want to answer this question separately for different 'chunks' of time; for example, you could divide it up into First year, Preschool, Primary term-time, Primary holidays and so on. How you describe the demands is entirely up to you.

TOP TIP

Some people find it helpful to base this exercise on the clock and to divide the time into hours and minutes for each task. This helps them work out what they can happily delegate, how much this might cost them and how much time they should allow for items they would prefer to do personally.

REAL-LIFE EXAMPLE

Baby's first year

Parent:
Important bonding time, for development.
Ensure a strong foundation.
Involvement of one of us with feeding and routines for most of every day.
Relaxed time for communication.
Possibly single other carer during first year – maximum of four hours per day, four days per week.

Spouse:
Allow time out for us. Two hours/week minimum.
Have time to share and listen properly, not stressed out and not exhausted.

Each of us having own time for gym or study each week – three hours per week.

Homemaker:
Be able to afford the mortgage on our wonderful house.
Have enough extra income for comfortable living.
Holidays abroad may go on hold for some years, but would be nice. Keep home clean and hygienic – four hours per week. Tidiness – 30 minutes per day.
Washing and ironing, seven hours per week.

Entertainer/educator:
Make plenty of fun, laughs and interest. Find toys, sights and sounds to stimulate.
Find suitable social environments to join in with regularly – four hours a week minimum.

Son's reception year

Parent:
One of us always picking up. School run: 30 minutes twice a day. Share and listen during after-school hours and at suppertime.
Able to have friends home – important for socialization.
Stimulating play and physical activity, getting involved with projects.

Spouse:
As above.

Homemaker:
Always have good stock of fresh fruit and vegetables, as much from the garden as possible.

Creating nice outdoor relaxing and playing area, one hour per day. Cook nutritious meals from scratch most evenings. Encourage family to sit down together to eat when possible.

Entertainer/educator:
Similar to above. Support his learning, especially reading practice – 30 minutes' dedicated time per evening.
French club if we can get him into it this year.
Swimming lessons – 45 minutes per week.

Daughter's year one

Parent:
As above.
Help out with French club at the school towards end of the year.

Spouse:
As above.

Homemaker:
Create a nice place to come back to: one hour per week. General shopping: two hours per week. Share small chores with children as appropriate.
Send to school with healthy snack.

Entertainer/educator:
Similar to above. Support her learning and homework this year and take an interest in what she is reading. 30 minutes dedicated time per evening. French and football clubs.
Swimming lessons – 45 minutes per week.

TOP TIP

Plan some time that you can spend by yourself and time that you can spend with your partner or close friends. Without these breaks, you risk becoming stressed and snappy and undoing all your good work in other areas. Time out is important for everyone, but especially for those juggling a career and family commitments, so don't think you're being selfish – you're not!

Step three:
Work out which demands are compatible

Now that you have the dual demands in your life laid out, you'll be in a better position to work out areas where your current role is compatible with them and areas where it is not. For example, you might want to be at home in time to pick the children up at 3pm each day, but you may be working in a role with a long commute that makes this impossible. Add up the time and work out whether this entire list can actually fit into the time available.

✔ Make the demands on your time more compatible with your available energy and resources by splitting up the demands so that they become more manageable and by getting help from others if you can. Be imaginative about this and think about solutions such as:

● getting extra help with the children from an extended family member;

- sharing the school run with a trusted friend;

- paying for help from a childminder, nanny, nanny-share or nursery;

- hiring a cleaner to help with housework, shopping and laundry;

- finding an au pair for help with the laundry and to babysit.

Step four:
Think about the advantages of not working

This chapter has started from the perspective of those who want to manage work and family together. You can go for a different route, though, and think about taking a career break and staying at home to handle family commitments if you have a partner who can provide the income. Here are some advantages to this solution:

- the higher earner continues to earn at his or her maximum level, giving the family the maximum income per hour worked;

- each of you has your area of focus with clearly delegated responsibilities and aren't stretched too thin;

- childcare may be so expensive that it all but wipes out the second income anyway;

- there is increased time and energy for looking after home, partner and family.

Common mistakes

 You don't negotiate

In general, employers are more enlightened in their approach to flexible working, especially after the business changes forced on them by the COVID-19 pandemic. However, they may not be aware of what your specific needs are and may need to be sold the advantages of the system you're proposing. It's often a good idea to write down what you're asking for, so that you can structure your argument well and also so that the recipient has time to digest the information and give a more considered answer. If the answer is no, ask what flexible arrangements would be acceptable and take the negotiation from there. If your employer is unwilling to consider any changes to your working arrangements, take advice about your position from an employment lawyer or from your trade union if you belong to one.

BUSINESS ESSENTIALS

✔ Start by identifying the demands that you face and what they might be in other roles.

✔ Think about which of these are compatible already and identify changes that will help you.

✔ Consider the advantages of working and make sure you weigh these up carefully against the advantages of a career break.

✔ Work out which childcare and home-help options could be right for you.

✔ Identify which working model will suit your family life now and in future years and decide how you can sell this to your employer.

✔ Be aware of your rights: your boss or company may not necessarily be up to speed with the latest developments in employment law! It's a fast-moving area.

✔ Make any requests in writing. This means that you can keep a record of what has been said and when and you're also giving the recipient time to think over what you're saying rather than having to reply on the hoof.

6
Thinking about the benefits of a career break

One way of adjusting your work–life balance in favour of your home life is to take a career break. There are many positive reasons to take some time away from your usual working day and its routine – a new parental role is the most common reason, but study, travel, trying out a business idea, bereavement or caring for a sick relative are other priorities that trigger people to spend a period away from work.

People may also take a break to get away from the aspects of their career that they enjoy least. Stress and pressure, office politics and turbulent periods of upheaval, like the COVID-19 pandemic, can cause all of us to look for a change of scene that allows us to recharge our batteries, look after our health and remind ourselves of what we really want in life.

If you've planned to take a career break, you've some options to think about once you get back; you might return to your old job or look for a new challenge when you're ready. These days, companies are more likely to look on career breaks favourably and indeed an enlightened employer may have a policy that goes far beyond statutory parental rights. Rather than lose the investment already made in your training and development, they'll agree to career breaks in the hope that their people will eventually return to employment with increased commitment, renewed loyalty, a broader perspective and additional skills.

Step one: Look at your motives

It's a good idea to step back and take some time to ask yourself why a career break holds such appeal for you. Do you know already what you hope to experience or achieve? What secondary or underlying objectives do you have?

 Visualize the beginning, middle and end of your time away and your eventual return to work. Make notes about how you want it to be in an ideal situation, but also think about how it might work realistically.

The main obstacles

Your other priorities are actually the main obstacles. The most common reasons for not taking a long career break are to do with:

- your partner;

- your family;

- your career;

- your house.

For most people, giving up work for a period of time means a loss of the income on which they have become dependent.

In general, the younger you are and the less routine your life is, the less inhibited you may feel in taking the plunge. At the other end of the spectrum, there are some lucky people for whom a career break of 12 or 24 months can be managed on savings alone, allowing them to return to pick up their previous routine without any material change.

TOP TIP

It is possible to be made redundant while on a career break, although your employer is expected to consult with you and your trade union in the usual way. If your employer decides to select you for redundancy solely because you're on a career break, this could be held to be unfair redundancy selection.

The length of time you've been working for your employer will have a bearing on the situation. If you have two years' continuous service, you're protected against unfair dismissal, including unfair selection for redundancy, and you're also entitled to a redundancy payment. A break of one week will break this continuity, except under circumstances where it's customary for such absence to count for continuity. If, therefore, you can show that absence on a career break constitutes such circumstances, you'd be protected. As this is a complex area, discuss it with your employer and ask for a statement about continuity to be added to any letters regarding your career break arrangements.

Step two:
Prepare to ask your employer

When you broach the issue with your boss, it's important to be clear in your mind about everything you want.

✓ Take along some notes as prompts if you'd find that helpful.

✓ Know what you're asking for, including the length of time away, pay and benefits, continuity of employment, possibility of return to the same role and so on.

To make the idea seem as attractive as possible, you need to be able to explain what benefits your break will bring both for you and your employer, and prepare a statement about wanting to return.

✓ Make a business case that would encourage your employer to support your request. For example, let's say that you work for a large multinational organization but that you'd like to spend some time abroad learning Spanish. You could say that the language skills you'd gain on your break would be put to good use when you return as you'd be able to liaise more quickly and effectively with your organization's branches in both Europe and Latin America.

TOP TIP

Remember that time off doing nothing may not only be hard to sell to your boss, but to prospective employers, too, if you plan on changing jobs upon your return. However, having and achieving some valuable personal objectives during your time away may well affect your career for the better. You'll often be perceived with respect (and perhaps a little jealousy) for having the initiative, confidence and determination to realize a dream. You'll need to make sure that you communicate what you've gained from your break clearly and positively, though. Stress the benefits when you describe what you've been doing and quantify your achievements if you can. For example, if you have management skills and you've been working overseas for a charity, you could say: 'I helped secure finance for a health centre which enabled it to take on three more members of staff and increase its impact in the community.'

You could also find out whether there's a policy that provides for sponsored sabbaticals. Your employer might be prepared to provide what you request or suggest a compromise.

✔ Be ready to be flexible and to meet your employer halfway. Remember that your request may have come completely out of the blue, so he or she may feel a bit 'ambushed'.

Step three:
Be ready in case the answer is 'no'

You have to be prepared for things not going to plan. If this does happen, first of all find out why you've been turned down. The provision of career breaks is purely at the discretion of your employer, but if they're made available only to certain people, then they're clearly behaving in a discriminatory manner. If other work colleagues have been granted similar time off for parental or study purposes and you haven't been supplied with a satisfactory explanation as to why you have not, you may want to claim a grievance through your HR department (if your company has one) or your union.

Even though you're bound to feel disappointed at first, look at the positive aspect of your company's decision: freedom. If you're that committed to the idea of the career break, you'll just go anyway, even if your employer won't keep your job open. The obvious downside to your employer agreeing to a break is that you're obligated to return.

You may feel very differently about that once you've been away for a while, so in a way you've been relieved of that decision.

Step four:
Consider other ways of achieving your goals

✓ Go part-time. Part-time work can free you up to realize your dreams without having to take such a significant drop in earnings. If you stay with the same employer, it can also give you continuity of routine and of your social network, both of which can help to reduce the stress related to big changes in your life.

✔ Take advantage of 'hybrid' working practices. Most companies, if practical for the role, now offer all employees the chance to work some of the time from home. This can allow you more time in your chosen environment and give you the flexibility to control when you work. Be aware that work will still eat up reasonably large chunks of your time and attention and you may feel isolated if you work from home all of the time. It may also mean that you can't spend as much time focusing on the new challenges you're hoping to explore.

✔ Work abroad. This can be a great way to satisfy a craving for novelty and variety while furthering your career ambitions at the same time. It's the best way to master a foreign language and to gain an understanding of a nation's culture, as you're totally immersed in it.

TOP TIP

Don't forget the financial benefits of working abroad: you'll still be earning something, so this is a good way to fund your itchy feet. You may choose to work within your usual field through a secondment or a change of employer or you may go for a complete change, such as picking grapes or teaching English. Remember that for most countries you'll have to apply for work permits/visas, some of which can be tricky to get hold of.

Whatever you do, make sure you have all the necessary documents before you travel to your chosen destination.

Change your employer. This can give you the chance to negotiate terms as part of your contract, with a view to a future break. This works for study breaks and for travel abroad but may not be suitable for parental breaks, the timescale for which may already be dictated!

If you (or your partner) are already expecting a baby, changing employer could result in a loss of rights to maternity pay, shared parental leave and statutory shared parental pay. For example, although currently all pregnant employees have a right to a year's maternity leave regardless of how long they have been employed, you can only receive statutory maternity pay (SMP) for up to 39 weeks if you have been employed by the same employer continuously for a minimum of 26 weeks into the 15th week before your due date. Similarly, statutory shared parental pay is only payable to those employed by the same employer continuously for a minimum of 26 weeks into the 15th week before your due date This may not affect your rights at the moment, but it's worth bearing in mind.

Looking for a new role on your return can give you complete freedom, and it's certainly a good option if you're hoping to take an extended career break. It may also be the most suitable route if you intend to retrain, take a completely new direction in your career or care for children or other family members in the long term.

Step five:
Take the plunge

Look back over the notes you took when you were daydreaming about your career break and prioritize

your objectives. Which are most important to you?
These are the 'core' of what you'll achieve.

✔ Think about the obstacles that may stand in your
way and the contingency plans you'll need to make
to deal with them. Obviously you can't see all the
potential events that may throw you off course, but
attempting to identify the most obvious will bring
your plan into the real world.

TOP TIP

Taking 12 months, for example, away from your
job will not generally leave you with a skills issue.
The more technical your role and the longer you
spend away from it, though, the more time and
effort you'll have to put into staying in touch.
Some employers, such as those in healthcare
professions, find it so important to retain good
workers that they'll not only allow them to take a
lengthy break but will also fund their skills updates
on their return. In other areas, it may be down to
you to update yourself. For more specific advice
on this area, talk to the relevant managers in your
company or organization or contact an industry
body for advice. If you belong to a trade union,
they may also be able to help.

✔ Assess the gap between where you are now and
where you want to be. Start breaking it up into
manageable chunks and then identify milestones
along the way. For example, if you're planning a
trip abroad, your first 'chunk' is research about

your destination(s), and the first milestone
is knowing which visas and work permits are
required.

Having a plan will help you move efficiently towards
your goals, but don't feel you have to stick to it rigidly.
You may decide to rethink your objectives as a result
of experiences you have early on, so try to remain
focused but be flexible, too. Once you get used to
planning in the way outlined above, you'll find you
waste less time worrying or dithering.

Step six:
Tie up loose ends

If you decide to leave your current job when you go on
your career break, make sure that you leave with the
best possible reputation so that you'll get a glowing
reference. This will also mean that you can apply to
your previous employer for work on your return, if you
so wish. If you are planning to return to the same role
after your break, it's even more important to make
sure that tasks are properly completed or handed over
efficiently and that you train your successor as well as
possible.

✔ Start making a list of important contacts and
duties well in advance of your leaving date to act
as a helpful resource to others in your absence. If at
all possible, set up a handover period so that your
successor can see what you do on an everyday
basis.

Common mistakes

✗ You don't keep in touch

Keeping in touch is vitally important if you want a smooth transition back into your previous role. It's also important if you'll be moving on to a new career. Stay attuned to who's who and catch up with relevant communications in your business or industry. This is easy to do these days, wherever you are. If you feel it's right for you, and you're taking some time out to complete a course of study, you could spend your holiday time back at work. This will help your finances as well as keep you in the 'loop'.

✗ You feel trapped by finances

Working out financial matters can be difficult and painful, but it can be done as long as you're absolutely clear about your priorities. For example, take time to identify where your money currently goes. What could you achieve with a different plan? Weigh up the benefits of continuing as you are, compared to what you might spend on your career break. Are there ways to reduce spending so that you can save for a career break in advance?

7
Learning to prioritize

Keeping control of tasks is an essential skill to master when you're trying to balance life and work. It will help you in all areas of life and is particularly useful if you decide to incorporate working from home into your new, better-balanced regime. Good prioritization helps you avoid distractions and become more efficient and self-reliant.

Some people naturally like structure in their life: 'control' is one of the 'big five' personality factors that psychologists agree on. If you're high on 'control' and enjoy structure, order and routines, it's unlikely that you'll struggle with the steps laid out below.

If, on the other hand, you prefer freedom and variety, you may feel constrained by structure and routines and find it harder to follow these steps. Persevere if you can, as you'll really reap some benefits. It might be a good idea to concentrate on using Step one, so that you're at least clear about what you're trying to achieve with your efforts.

Learning to prioritize frees up a lot of time for whatever you would prefer to be doing. Use the steps below as a framework and schedule imaginatively, to give you the variety you need in your daily life.

Step one:
Decide on your objectives

If you start off by being clear about what you want to achieve, the chances are that you'll succeed brilliantly. There are several levels to this step:

- What do you (personally) want to get out of any particular period of work (say a month, six months)?

- What do your boss/team/clients/company need you to achieve during this time?

- What specific goals do you want to have achieved by the end of this month?

✔ Write the answers to these questions on a sheet of A4. Hang them in a prominent place in your office, ideally where a distracted eye will fall. You can add on an adjacent sheet of A4 for your objectives for life outside work, if you feel inclined to.

You'll probably have several answers for each question, because our objectives are usually plural. If this is the case, you'll need to identify the relative importance of each element of your answer; it may help to organize your page with the most important elements first. Next to these will be the answers to the following questions, which it will become habitual to write at the beginning of the working week and day.

What do you need to get done by the end of this week?

What do you need to get done today?

These simple questions will light beacons to guide you through the chaos of each day. When faced with requests or demands for your time and attention, ask yourself how they will help you towards your objectives:

● Should I do it now or after more important objectives have been met?

● Is this something I need to deal with today?

● Is this something I need to deal with this week?

● Do I need to sort it out this month?

● Can this go right on the end of my list in case I have time?

● Should I bother with this at all?

● Can I delegate this to someone else?

Step two:
Use tools to help you

Although you don't want to clutter up your life even further, there are some tools that can help you live according to your priorities.

Diary

A diary helps you to plan ahead, scheduling specific dates or times for tasks and actions appropriately. It helps you to structure time towards deadlines so that you can monitor interim goals more easily and make sure they're met, with your ultimate goal being to deliver the outcome you want on time.

✓ Divide projects and objectives into constituent parts and place 'milestones' in your diary. Don't forget to schedule in time to meet people as well as time to complete key tasks, or you could risk isolating yourself.

A diary is especially useful to structure your time if you have lots of short meetings or telephone calls or if you need long chunks of time to focus on difficult, complex or creative work. By communicating your need to your colleagues and concentrating meetings and other work into one section of the day or week, you free yourself to work in a more effective manner.

Diaries are available in multiple formats: on paper, on the Internet, on your phone, and only you can know which one functions best for you. Whilst online and onscreen versions are shareable across devices, it is worth noting that a paper diary still does the job and is unlikely to develop technical trouble, run out of power or be incompatible with other systems.

To-do list

In its simplest form, a to-do list is a place to record the things you need to do, so that you can tick them off as you achieve them. Again, there are multiple ways and places to create, share and use them online but a simple paper list is also fine.

If you're aware that you take on too many tasks, a to-do list may help you to visualize your workload and manage requests more assertively. The most important thing to remember when using a to-do list is your objectives.

✓ Next to each entry on your list give the task a number to reflect the priority of the task relative to your objectives and the other tasks. You can even make your list public so that your boss and colleagues can see the work already assigned and do some of the prioritizing for you.

Time audit

This is a backwards look at how you've been spending your time. It's a useful tool to monitor how well you're focusing your time on the objectives you want to achieve.

✓ Looking back through your diary and to-do list, estimate the amount of time that you spent working towards the objectives you set yourself. Do the same for your time and objectives outside work. How does your time allocation tally? What needs to change: your objectives and priorities or your time management?

Project planner

When managing projects, a project planning system can help you to break down a complex system easily into its constituent elements, identify milestones, assign tasks to others and keep track of progress. Again, only you can know if you prefer to do this on paper or onscreen and which software package or app works best for you.

TOP TIP

'Prioritize' is a verb. That means action, not tools. People can have a very fancy toolkit to help them sort themselves out, but it'll be no use at all unless they actually do something with it. Don't fool yourself that having a diary and a to-do list means that you're organized. Even filling them in will not help alone. It's the discipline of following the schedule in your diary and focusing on the completion of each task on the to-do list that will make you efficient and successful.

Step three:
Manage your inputs and outputs

The process of working efficiently comes in managing the inputs as they happen and remaining focused on the output of the most important and urgent task.

First and most important: be clear which set of objectives you should be focused upon now – work or home objectives. If and when you work from home, separate your work space from your home space as far as you can. Separate work time from home time, work phone from home phone, and work email from home email, too. This way, you can protect yourself from the stress of role confusion.

Managing output

Here is a checklist of things to do when you start your work time.

- ✓ Look up at your objectives on the wall to focus you on what you need to achieve.

- ✓ Look at your diary and see what you've scheduled and how much time you have spare.

✓ Look at your to-do list and pick out the tasks that are most important and urgent. You can choose to start a long task and finish it on a different day or you may prefer to pick a single task that will fit within the time you have available.

✓ Allow yourself time for interruptions and three or four 10-minute breaks and a longer meal break within a working day. You'll be more focused and effective if you stay fresh. Now you can write your objectives for the day.

Managing input

✓ Make your days more efficient by allocating time slots to mail (digital and paper) and phone calls that need returning.

How you do this will depend on your role, but for most people, for example, the post will only need attention once a day, if at all. Emails carry the expectation that they'll be seen and dealt with immediately and some may generate more interruptions if left too long – you'll be chased by the people who sent you the initial message, for example. On the other hand, very few roles require people to respond to each email as soon as it arrives.

✓ Sort out your emails (and post, if necessary) as follows:

- junk: delete or bin immediately;

- items for reference: file them after opening everything;

- items to deal with now: respond to each one quickly and efficiently;

- items requiring more attention: add to your to-do list or schedule specific time in your diary.

Don't forget to think about how important each item is to the achievement of your objectives.

✓ Turn off your notifications as they will distract you each time you get a new message and allocate a maximum of three slots in the day for responding to email. Early morning mail may be urgent, so start the day with a quick check, check again after lunch and then one last time as you finish work for the day.

How you deal with your phones depends on your role. You may be expected to answer immediately during office hours. Perhaps you prefer to have the variety of contact with others throughout the day and enjoy the social side of the interruption. Some calls may be quickly dealt with if answered immediately, saving yourself and others time.

✓ If your role allows it, try to switch voicemail on and return calls during allocated slots through the day, as you did with emails. Doing this will allow you greater focus on your objectives for the day, making you more productive. You will need to get into the habit of regularly checking and returning calls, though.

Common mistakes

✗ Your standards drop over time

You owe it to yourself to put in a full and focused day towards your objectives or it's unlikely that you'll meet them. If it helps, imagine your boss or colleague's reaction to a piece of work you're finishing. Does it do you justice?

BUSINESS ESSENTIALS

✓ Know what you're trying to achieve. Break down large or vague objectives into smaller and more manageable chunks, making them more achievable. If you have trouble doing this, get help from your boss or a business coach.

✓ Keep the correct set of objectives in mind at all times.

✓ Know your tools and how to use them. If in doubt about how to use a particular technology, get some training to learn how to make the most of it.

✓ Build your own way of managing inputs and outputs, based upon the suggestions in this section, into your routine. Have a schedule that helps you and stick to it.

✓ Be clear about your different roles and try to keep them separate. There will be times when you're required to switch between them but don't allow this to become routine.

✓ If you find you're slipping back into your old haphazard methods, return to this section regularly to remind yourself. If you struggle at first, have faith! Anyone can learn to prioritize but it may take some time for it to become habitual.

8
Surviving stress

Regardless of the general balance of your life, there will be times that are stressful. Learning the practical steps to cope with stress is important to help you get through these episodes. It isn't recommended that you accept and try to cope with an everyday pattern of stress over a long period of time, since this can be very detrimental to your health. Get the balance right first and take steps to deal with stress comfortably.

Step one:
Identify the main sources of stress

Pressure can be positive, providing challenges and building confidence as you achieve them. How you see the situation can make the difference between whether you experience pressure or stress. It's important to understand which situations you're finding stressful and to identify the elements within them that cause the stress. General sources of stress at work, home and in balancing different roles are:

- conflict between people;
- handling difficult behaviour;
- performance worries;

- demanding routines;
- increased requirements on your attention or time;
- financial worries.

Identify sources of everyday stress that fit into each of these categories for you and work out how you can eliminate or alleviate it.

Major life changes have also been shown to cause a disproportionate amount of stress, especially where three or more occur within the same two-year period. The most stressful life events are:

- death of your partner;
- divorce or separation;
- legal proceedings against you;
- a prison term;
- personal injury;
- marriage;
- having/adopting a baby;
- losing/changing jobs;
- retirement;
- moving home;
- death of family member.

Think about the life events that have affected you in the last two years. The process of adapting to these will inevitably take a toll on your welfare, as you understand, respond to and live with the change. Think about each life event and how you've dealt with it but without dwelling too much upon it. Give yourself plenty of relaxation time for recovery, using it to do something that you enjoy, unrelated to the change you're facing. Many people will be going through similar life changes. Even those who aren't can understand that this is a difficult time for you and will want to help, so don't isolate yourself.

Step two:
Sort out stressful relationships

Contact with others is crucial for getting things done at work, but some people are a lot easier to deal with than others.

Your support network outside work can help you to deal with pressures and actually reduce your stress, so getting relationships in good working order is well worth doing.

Criticism

Do you have to put up with a constant stream of criticism or put-downs from one person? People who are always negative about you or your ideas are probably feeling insecure. Reminding others of their faults is used to deflect attention from their own perceived failings. Perhaps they feel their position is threatened or that they need to compete with you. People like this may feel frustrated or have low self-esteem and they often don't like to see others enjoying success or higher self-esteem than them.

✓ When someone makes a personal attack, rise above it and remain cheerful, rather than reacting to it negatively.

✓ Use phrases such as 'that's an interesting perspective' to show that you've heard without agreeing.

✓ Repeat back a negative comment to the person
who gave it. Very often they'll notice the destruct-
ive effect of their words and will tone down what
they've said about you or qualify it. Listen carefully,
as this could be useful feedback. Perhaps you've
said or done something that they find difficult to
cope with.

✓ When your critic uses sarcasm, interpret what
they're saying to check what they're implying and
then ask 'Why do you say that?' to clarify their
meaning. This also highlights their negative tactics,
which may be enough to stop the behaviour.

✓ Confront persistent critics directly. Describe the criticism you've been receiving, disclose how it makes
you feel, suggest what you would like instead. 'You
have been sarcastic and critical of me on a number
of occasions recently, which I find hurtful. If you
have a problem with something I do, come and tell
me direct so we can discuss it'.

✓ At work, make a log of events, including your attempts to confront and resolve the problem.

Anger

Do you cope well with angry people? Here are a
few simple tips that will help you to draw positive
outcomes from difficult situations.

✓ Keep calm yourself, concentrate on breathing
slowly, listening carefully and keeping your body
language open.

✓ Disarm the immediate mood by responding and showing concern: 'I can see that this has really upset you; let's discuss it so I can understand fully and see what we can do about it'.

✓ If someone is too upset to listen there's little point wasting your energy. Ask them to come back when they've calmed down so that you can discuss their problem properly.

✓ Find a good time and place to discuss persistent anger problems. Warn the people concerned first about what you want to discuss, so they can prepare themselves. Work out why the person uses inappropriate behaviour, what they hope to gain or what their angry tactics have won for them before. Plan what you'll say to them before you challenge their difficult behaviour. Remind yourself they may have a real grievance or frustration that you can deal with.

✓ Describe your observations of the problem and why it causes problems for you and/or others. Explain what you want them to stop and what you would like to see instead. Ask them if there are any problems with making this change and discuss what you can do to help them. Compromise and negotiation may be required for a solution.

Dead battery

Can you identify people in your life who act as a dead battery, draining you of your energy whilst giving little in return? Sometimes we can simply 'unhook' ourselves from a negative or an unresponsive person and have less to do with them. It can be difficult or impossible to do this if they're in our work team or family. The issue has to be dealt with rather than avoided. Find or create a good time to talk to them, preferably with just the two of you and no distractions. Describe your observations of their behaviour and disclose how it makes you feel. Explain what you think would make the situation better and ask them if there are any barriers to that happening.

Real-life example

Harry finds that Peter's withdrawal from usual family conversations worries him. His attempts to include his son in what he is doing or to get conversations going are met with negativity or silence. Harry worries. Peter is clearly unhappy and the problem is affecting the family atmosphere. Harry sends the rest of the family out on an errand. He describes to Peter what he has noticed and how worried it has made him feel. He describes Peter's former positive outlook and how great it was to be with him.

Harry asks if there's anything getting in the way of a return to this. They discuss a particular problem that is affecting Peter at school and how to deal with it. Though Harry feels that Peter held a lot back in their conversation, the progress was a relief and the atmosphere was immediately better.

Step three:
Communicate assertively

Prioritization and self-organization can reduce your stress and help you to manage a demanding workload. In a nutshell, promising less can mean that you get more done but what if you find it hard to say no or to ask for the help you need? As with any skill, practice improves performance, so here are some exercises that will improve your ability to assert yourself.

✓ Be assertive in your body language. Stand (or sit) tall, taking up plenty of space. Breathe deeply and easily, making eye contact with an open expression. Don't fiddle with your hands or cross your arms or legs. Clasp your hands lightly, relaxing your shoulders.

✓ Practise projecting your voice strongly. Start by exhaling all the air in your lungs, which will trigger your body to take a deep breath before you talk. Enunciate consonants clearly, keep your voice soft but turn up the volume. Drop the pitch of your voice (without dropping the volume) at the end of the phrase to convey your conviction in your own words.

✓ Until you get used to communicating assertively, you may want to give yourself time to consider your response with useful phrases like 'Possibly, I'll get back to you on that' or 'I need to think about that, I'll let you know'.

✓ If people interrupt you while you're talking, raise a hand to signal 'stop', increase the volume slightly and finish your sentence with conviction. If this continues to happen, you can say 'please let me finish' as you put up your hand, to draw the person's attention to what they're doing. Keep your cool and continue your point, 'I was saying that...'

✔ Recognize the other's point of view whilst saying what you think. It's important to express yourself honestly but constructively. A useful phrase could be: 'I realize that you...but I feel that...'

✔ When asked to do something, state clearly what your answer is, what you're prepared to do and what you are not. Don't feel that you have to justify yourself; it's the request that you're turning down, not the person. Repeat the message until the other person accepts it and don't be browbeaten.

TOP TIP

Believe in the value of your perspective and opinions: they are valuable. Remind yourself: 'there are many perspectives on any situation and my point of view is worth hearing; people may need my perspective, too'.

Step four:
Develop stress-busting habits

Biochemicals are released in response to stress to prepare your body for action. If 'fight' or 'flight' aren't required to deal with the situation they may continue to affect the whole body even after the stress has gone. Taking exercise as part of the working day is the single most effective stress-reliever. Regular exercise boosts your energy and gives you increased stamina. It removes the effects of the biochemicals adrenaline and cortisol. Exercise will relieve stress: following a stressful meeting, take a brisk walk to burn them off before resuming your day.

A routine that includes aerobic, anaerobic and stretching exercises is ideal but the best exercise of all is the kind that fits in with your lifestyle. A walk to work, a policy of using the stairs rather than the lift and a lunchtime stroll are ways to fit exercise into the working day. A Saturday cycle ride and a couple of visits to the gym or exercise class during the week are all it takes to release the noradrenaline and endorphins, which relieves the tension caused by a frenetic daily routine. You'll improve your circulation and digestion at the same time, making a good night's sleep more likely.

TOP TIP

Agree with your partner or friends when you want to spend time together and then block it out in the diary. An exercise class is a good idea since it occurs at a set time and it's a good social activity if you enjoy time with others. Even if you spend a relaxing hour in the bath with some candles and a book, you'll feel more ready to handle the demands of others.

Say goodbye to 'false friends'. Cigarettes, coffee, alcohol and chocolate are all likely to add to the negative effects of stress over time. Give them up and get some help if you need it.

Common mistakes

 You're available 24/7

Deal with phones and emails during set periods of the day only. Turn off notifications on your computer/mobile and turn off your phone in-between times so that you can concentrate on other things. This still means that you're giving people a reasonable response time but in managed chunks of time that will keep you sane.

 You don't prioritize your emails

With emails, a full inbox can be overwhelming, so start with a trawl through to delete spam and other unimportant 'noise'. Then 'classify' the emails that remain: some require an instant response and some require only a couple of lines and can be dispatched straight away. File longer emails that require your considered response or ones with reading matter attached, so that you can give them appropriate attention; make a quick note in your to-do list to remind you. Prioritize the mails that are left and deal with them as effectively as you can.

BUSINESS ESSENTIALS

✓ Recognize stressful situations and try to plan ahead for them. Identify what you can do to help yourself.

✓ Major life events can knock you for six, especially where several occur in the same two years. Don't isolate yourself – contact with others will help you get back on your feet.

✓ When dealing with difficult behaviour, keep a positive outlook; getting down or angry will not help the situation.

✓ Confront people who are consistently difficult and try to get the relationship on a healthier footing. Describe what the problem is, describe how it affects you and others, describe what you would like to see and ask what the barriers are.

✓ Know what you want and communicate it assertively. Expect a positive reaction and you'll very often get one if what you're asking for is fair.

✓ Develop healthy habits of exercise and eating. Being in shape will allow you to live life to your full potential.

Where to find more help

Government services and information gov.uk

If you want to find out about employment rights in the UK, including details on flexible working, parental leave and redundancy, this is the best place to start.

BBC Worklife
bbc.com/worklife/tags/work-life-balance

The BBC offers information on all aspects of working life, from the practical to the philosophical.

Mental Health Foundation mentalhealth.org.uk/a-to-z/w/work-life-balance

Some great resources and insight into what causes stress and how to re-balance your life.

The 4-Hour Workweek: Escape 9-5, Live Anywhere and Join the New Rich

Timothy Ferriss, Harmony, 2010

Tim Ferriss is a Silicon Valley entrepreneur, writer and broadcaster. This, his first book, asks how we can make the most of our time, and our money, to live the life we want. A classic.

Off Balance: Getting Beyond the Work-Life Balance Myth to Personal and Professional Satisfaction

Matthew Kelly, Hudson Street Press, 2011

Rather than strive for balance, Kelly argues we should strive for satisfaction, in both life and work. We cannot, he says, separate life and work and balance one against the other; instead we should seek to find fulfilment in each one.

Work like a Woman: A Manifesto for Change

Mary Portas, Bantam Press, 2018

An impassioned discussion of what working life is like for women and how it should and could change, written by one of the UK's most high-profile businesswomen. Full of business advice, tips and suggestions for a new working culture.

Index

BUSINESS ESSENTIALS